DUETS

Praise for Tikuli's Poetry Books
available from Leaky Boot Press

Collection of Chaos

Tikuli's full blooded new book of poetry *Collection of Chaos* is too good to be missed. Her poems are direct and strong and I would not want to be on the wrong end of one of them. But when the occasion demands her writing is heartbreakingly tender and you'll want to put your arms around her.

John Lyle (Canadian singer-songwriter)

Collection of Chaos is the perfect title for Tikuli's impressive collection of poems. Dealing subjects as varied as human condition womanhood, nature, hope and loss – to name a few – each poem rings true with experience and thought. …Tikuli proves that we have much to expect from this horizon, not to mention a lot to learn. *Collection of Chaos* is thus not only a fantastic collection, but also an important one, as it places life back where it lies, in the heart of chaos.

Sebastian Doubinsky (author, editor, academic)

For those who enjoy structural unconventionality in poetry coupled with bold issues usually made invisible, this book offers a most mature poetry. For those who like it lyrical and light, the verses on nature will leave a permanent impression on your minds… each poem of this book is like a world in itself – offering you thoughts to think and maybe ideas to pen even.

Sakshi Nanda (journalist/book critic, columnist, editor and blogger)

Wayfaring

Tikuli is a skilled *plein air* painter; her palette of words is spare, meticulously chosen and applied in a variety of metrical patterns that, while not avant-garde, are modernist and reliable. The reader is never required to study her metrics; her focus is on the act of recollection and its requisite imperative. She has stories to tell, portraits to paint, ghosts to address, and issues to redress.

Djelloul Marbrook (author and poet) in The Arabesques Review

I think this is a beautiful collection of poetry that brings me the sounds, sights and smells of an exotic land. There is a train ride that I will never forget. Tikuli shares her heart and heartbreak. These are poems of observation, of ritual, of being a mother, being a lover and survival in every sense of the word. In these poems, the poet bares her beautiful soul.

Matthew Bailer (poet, painter, photographer)

DUETS

COLLABORATIVE POEMS BY
TIKULI &
JAMES GODDARD

LEAKY BOOT PRESS

Duets
by Tikuli and James Goddard

First published in 2018 by
Leaky Boot Press
http://www.leakyboot.com

Copyright © 2018 Tikuli
Copyright © 2018 James Goddard
All rights reserved

No part of this book may be reproduced or transmitted in any form or by any means, electronic, mechanical, photocopying, recording, or otherwise, without prior written permission of the author.

ISBN: 978-1-909849-67-9

Contents

Introduction: How & Why	9
Lingering	11
Mended	12
Dialogue	13
Knowing	14
Star-Music	15
Paper Boats	16
Forest	17
Restless	18
Dust Motes	19
The Raven	20
The Garden (1)	21
The Garden (2)	22
Illusion	23
Dinner	24
Petals	25
Reminiscence	26
Hallucinations	27
Stone Ghosts	29
Gone	30
The Garden	31
Lakeside	32
Lost	33
Poetry	34

Marking	35
Shadow-Cat	36
Day-Night	37
Drought	38
Moxie	39
Museum	40
Nocturne	41
Reverberations	43
Farmer	44
Leaving	46
Tree	47
Windows	48
Soliloquy	50
Streets	51
Dawn	52
Unpunctuated	53
Lost Gods	54
Vowels	56
Mud	58
Reflections	59
Memories of Snow	60
Night-Watch	61
The Path	62
Streetlife	63
Night Ballad	64
Morning	66
Seasons (1)	67
Seasons (2)	68
Monochrome (1)	69
Monochrome (2)	70
Stories	71
Still Life (1)	72
Still Life (2)	73
Coadunation	74

Stone Ghosts   75
Wondering   76
Chiaroscuro   77
Pavane   78
Alphabet Soup   79
Seascape   80
Desolation   81
Stardust   82
Daybreak   83

Introduction: How & Why

Perhaps it is a myth that writing poetry is a lonely art.

Collaborations among poets have a long history and in these days of the internet it has become easier to collaborate than ever before—using text messages, email or even working on the same poem while living thousands of miles apart. These poems came into being through our conversations on Facebook messenger.

When we first decided to write together we also decided that we would post the poems alternately on Facebook. Whoever wrote the first line, which we took turns in doing, would be the one to post. Lines were then added, turn and turn-about, until we were both satisfied that the poem was complete. We then individually edited our text into a final form, and then, before posting, we decided which version worked best. Sometimes we couldn't agree and we kept both versions, but this was rare. When we began these collaborations neither of us imagines that they would become a book. We did it for fun and posted for friends to read.

It was both exciting and liberating to watch new poems emerge as pieces developed. We allowed the poems to lead us, to find their own form, rather than forcing a form upon them—this was a strangely intimate experience. Words are portals and we saw this during our writing of these poems; suddenly a new line would redirect our thought processes to somewhere quite unexpected. We both had to try to accommodate wordplay and word usages that were not our own, a way of thinking that was alien to us. We each had to recognise the other's unique voice and be comfortable with it as well as startled and surprised by it. Sometimes we found that not being in total control gave us the strength to break mental barriers and create something beautiful and unexpected.

It's amazing how these impromptu collaborative works grew organically into a form challenging the role, gender, age, personality, culture which are usually the mark of one's individual work. Here all bets are off. We trusted each other and took the many directions the words steered us into without being judgemental about what the other had written.

What we love most about our work is how this exercise blurred individual lines. When reading the poem here one could not really point out who wrote which line—and that is something beautiful.

The joy in creating something together is immeasurable. Time was a big challenge as both of us are writers with large workloads, but we somehow managed to hold on to what we were doing and assigned times to get together online to write new pieces and enjoy our collaborative time together.

As for the title of this book, for that we thank our friend Sabine who was the first to call these pieces 'duets'.

Tikuli
New Delhi, India

James Goddard
Yorkshire, England

August, 2018

Lingering

she lives in a house of mirrors
reflecting darkness not light
she moves like a shadow at night

her inner blackness glows
and throbs where her heart would beat
if life had not deserted her

she was ancient like stones
and the bones of the long dead
as ageless as a year of yesterdays

in her lifeless house of mirrors
wrapped in the folds of time
she dwells forgotten and alone

dark memories haunt her darkness
as just a shifting blur she lingers
in the dark corners of time.

Mended

broken walls and broken windows
broken lives and broken shadows
memories you can't remember
times in life like glowing embers
recalled things we did together
things we did that were so tender
as we our differences dismembered
and to fate we both surrendered
as we took to our marriage bed

Dialogue

do you believe in time travel
probably not, but we can pretend
why? we all time travel every day
but time is just a human concept
our humanity lets us travel through time
surely time is only a perception
does that matter? art is only a perception
you mean we travel through art too?
yes, and through music, hate, love...
it's an illusion that exists only through us
which—time, love, hate, music, art or this poem?
all of them are fantasies born out of timelessness
everything is a fantasy born out of time
time itself is a fantasy
fantasy itself is of time
and we travel from one to another?
fantasy we carry with us, time we travel through
time is a swing door, so is this poem
this poem is a see-saw... it has its ups and downs
swaying between probability & possibility
swaying between possibility & inevitability
swaying between rational mind and infinite mind
swaying from the irrational to the irrational
maybe that's what a vague mind calls time travel
no, most of us know we are passing through time
what makes you so certain about that?
the nature of the experiences we all undergo
oh! I think we've run out of time... goodbye!

Knowing

the forest is quiet tonight
darkness is all around
rolled contours of shadows
create a landscape of dreams
in the stillness of night
something forgotten stirs
a memory rises in the waters
that wash across my mind
a scent from the past comes
spectres ride down moonbeams
the air hums a sad tune
as mists swallow the stars
soft as autumn rain my tears fall
each one a distant memory
grieving trees shed their leaves
as, like me, nature weeps
my melancholy grows as I remember
and finally know that you are gone

Star-Music

I remember my tree in our garden
that grew higher than the moon
its leaves glowing with celestial crimson
whispered in the night-time breeze
the blossoms filled with the scent of you
gave life to long forgotten memories
that echoed with the songs of nothingness
cosmic star-music vast and empty
then one summer night the lightening came
and burned all life from its ancient wood
my tree became like night's consoling dark
until the morning when I saw its ash
grey and snow-like, sad upon the earth.

Paper Boats

Paper boats upon the water
Palimpsests all folded up
always hiding the whole story
hidden words and messages
tales of dreams and struggles
written, effaced, and defaced
to conceal the lies in truth
or conceal the truth in lies
a haunting graffiti floating
on the ocean's restless body
lost words dissolved in water
where suffusing the Earth
with word-pictures of the love
and bloodshed of times past
they will add their contagion
of lore to all that is yet to be
then paper boats upon the water
will carry tales of good and bad
across the endlessly moving sea
that first carried them to me

Forest

a stream in an ancient forest
gathering history as it flows
its wandering waters restless
for when they reach the sea
primeval trees stretch above
its haunted past like sentinels
guarding a gate to the present
moon licked, the water circles
the ivy clad ruins of lost cities
from before the age of man
built by gods or monsters
or nature's shaping hands
twilight moves through them
swirling the dust of aeons
into new configurations
these are the ruins of dark
these are the ruins of time
a land of buried memories
shaped by the tireless waters
that scour the land for fragments
things so long obscured
thing so long forgotten
things for the minds of men
whose time has at last come
the forest listens to their voices
making sounds it has never known

Restless

a creaking door wide open
reveals the other side
of either light or darkness—
forgotten shadows in between
that walk alone at night—
autumn's wind haunts me
and whistles in the trees
the music of a banshee—
I—possessed by the house
that haunts the house
that haunts my dreams—
pull the duvet to my chin
and wait to lose the fears
within my tired mind
darkness reaches out for me
softly calls a name, my name
just as I recall the darkness
from within me came
I drift between the dark
and deeper dark
until the morning comes
when outside I hear rain
hissing like bacon cooking
in a backstreet cafe
I curse and light a cigarette
at last I start to dress
my fear is gone until I rest again

Dust Motes

Those days are only snapshots now,
Faces I've forgotten, faded colours,
Memories, transient on an autumn breeze,
Each one a fallen leaf that lived and died,
Mementos of so many things we did
In that distant time we lived as one.
Our non-existent universe of love,
Grey seas and iridescent daydreams,
Vanished in the soft mists of morning,
Terracotta sunsets, bright moonlight,
Myriad stars above, the coldness of space,
I saw them as a slowly changing slideshow
Projected by the happiness I felt—
Now, we are only motes, life's final dust,
Riding on the dying breath of others,
Lost between somewhere and nowhere
Yearning, seeking what is missing,
A sense of me, a sense of you, a sense of us.
One day the scent of spring will come,
Then we will fly together once again.

The Raven

a raven comes, sits by my side
pecks me with its raptor beak
then turns its beady eyes on me
and asks 'friend, what is it you seek?'
'a mug of coffee smoking hot
so make it black and not too sweet'
'in which case I will fly away'
for coffee sire I cannot make'
'oh no, Mr. Raven please do stay.'
'no, now I don't wish to play'
'perhaps we'll meet another day'
'Well if you must go then good day'
'Goodbye,' he says, and spreads his wings
and soars into the sun-filled sky

The Garden (1)

In the pergola of dying plants
a tendril sleeps unnoticed
by the diseased dogs that prowl,
above, a vulture waits to feast
among the bodies of the dead,
nearby, a stream tries to breathe
as ornamental fish suffocate
in its stagnant waters,
stunted trees breathe heavy
in the polluted afternoon air,
vines cling to the garden walls
drawing moisture from the mortar
as the ancient wall collapses
a straggling fence around the ruins,
its iron twisted and rusting,
gravestone studded, grassless lawns
littered with broken coffin-wood,
wind echoes around the ancient stones,
around so much sad decay,
among all this, memory haunts,
seeking something that is lost
never finding

During the writing of these collaborations we both produced a version of what we thought the finished poem should be and then selected the one we both preferred. Occasionally we coudn't agree; in those few cases we give both versions here.

The Garden (2)

in the pergola of dying plants
a tendril sleeps unnoticed
by the diseased dogs that prowl;
overhead, a vulture waits to feast
among the bodies of the dead,
nearby, a stream tries to breathe
as ornamental fish suffocate
in its diseased waters,
stunted trees inhale heavily
of the poisoned afternoon air,
vines clinging to the garden walls
drawing moisture from the mortar
as the ancient wall collapses,
a straggling fence around the ruins,
its overgrown iron rusting,
gravestone studded, grassless lawns
littered with broken coffin-wood,
a wind moans around this place,
around so much decay—
among all this, four feet walking,
a couple as silent as the dead,
they hold hands, they smile,
as they forget why they are here.

During the writing of these collaborations we both produced a version of what we thought the finished poem should be and then selected the one we both preferred. Occasionally we couldn't agree; in those few cases we give both versions here.

Illusion

summer noon, dreamy heat
sand beneath my unshod feet
rain riding on grey clouds
driven back by warming sun
dust rising from the earth
carries history in its motes
birds silent, in their shelters
keep cool while I swelter
gloom distant in the sky
but it can't displace the light
trees in anticipation
of the time of mists and fruit
feel a day so still and quiet
afternoon has now begun
the soft riffling of a breeze
imparts life into the world
I feel drops of summer rain
then I wonder if they're real
so they disappear again
taking all that is so good
in this illusive world I made

Dinner

only tears would clean the stains
hunger left on her face
as she tried to understand
what was wrong with the rich
and decadent food she ate
as unsatisfying as lost love
it left her gaunt and empty
her starved reflection stared at her
from the shine of her empty plate
absentmindedly her finger
traced the contours
of the plate's cracked surface
as she dreamed of better times
twilight gathered in her eyes
and fed her inner darkness
soon the starless night would come
and invisible in the night
her empty plate might fill

Petals

the seasons have lost their magic
angry storm clouds are massing
the bare hills stare at the roiling sky
in the valley the river runs red
with the blood of centuries
wind howls between the hills
singing a tuneless song of loss
beside the river a poppy blooms
its petals lonely in this tortured land
ephemeral beauty, a poem of hope
poppy-red sails blow in the breeze
I tread in the dust of a million years
I leave my footprints to history
in my memory a train whistle calls
its sound duets with the wind
the clouds rupture, rain begins to fall
the river rises and overflows
I smile as I see the poppy sail away

Reminiscence

on the shelf a jar of marbles
gleams with childhood memories
and the games I played
each one with a meaning
a special time I remember well
now they gaze like empty eyes
upon a different world
where did the days go
when all we did was play?
when did we lose it all
the things that used to be?
what cast the spell on seasons
of enchanted rain, glorious summers
fireflies and autumnal woods?
what masked the scents of spices
gingerbread and spruce
that aren't what they seemed?
I miss the crackling fire
around which we stole a kiss
the old oafish ways, the sundress
the dandelions on which we wished
now all I have is a hushed spring
and memories of a lost world
yawning dawns and quiet streets
and days rolling into nights
memories shift like marbles
they roll inside my head
until I quite forget
what is real and what imagined
and yet... and yet... and yet..

Hallucinations

I have a jar of marbles
they glitter on the shelf
with memories of other days
and the games I played
each has a special meaning
a reminder of a season
when I was so much younger
than I am today
now their opaque eyes gaze
upon a different world
where innocence is lost—
and things that used to be
are forgotten in the past—
when summertime was long
with enchanted weather
we ate magic mushrooms
we found in the woods
we saw pumpkin spice
gingerbread and spruce
even castles made of ice
and gilded unicorns too
we sat around a fire
whose crackle I still crave
smoking and telling jokes
in our oafish way
I thought I was like Zebedee
bouncing on a spring
sometimes on the ground
I bounce and bounce around
sometimes in the air

but I know there's no spring there
between ten and eighteen
so much living is packed in
it all becomes as one
a continuum of images
whose timeline is forgot
so I take one of the marbles
I roll it on the ground
then I pause and watch it
going round and round
it mixes up my memories
until I quite forget
what is real and what made up
and yet... and yet... and yet...

During the writing of these collaborations we both produced a version of what we thought the finished poem should be and then selected the one we both preferred. Occasionally we coudn't agree; in those few cases we give both versions here. 'Reminisence' on the previous page and 'Hallucinations' are two such poems.

Stone Ghosts

I reach out and touch the walls,
feel marks on crumbling stones,
wonder where the people went
who once made this their home

while these ruins whisper tales
of life and loss in ancient times,
deep sorrow clings to them
like vines eclipsing history

they drink the echoes of the past,
in torpid, hot afternoon sun
that I feel burning on my back,
as this place weeps its loneliness

I heard the murmur of my heart
when I came to this desert ruin,
long-dead voices called to me
from unremembered walls

now I watch the orphaned stones,
as like sentinels they sit,
silently undead dreams still linger,
but find no resolution now

pale ghosts emerge between the walls,
then disappear into my thoughts,
as fine dust settles in the cracks,
as night-time drags me slowly home

Gone

the shadows of your memories
have rolled up and withdrawn
into the shell of regret you carry

things fell apart soundlessly
like decaying autumnal leaves
until nothing but shadows were left

now they too are gone from me
leaving only my emptiness
as a memorial to our longing

The Garden

I stroll in the garden of tortured trees,
where claw like branches reach to the sky
as if stretching for clouds to wring,
green moss creeps up their trunks
like sodden upholstery waiting to dry,
exposed roots erupt from the earth
to explore the windswept land,
as I listen to the stillness echoing
within the walls my grandfather built.

As clouds escape and drift away,
as sunshine flows across the ground,
ants emerge from quiet corners,
drawn to the decaying body of a bird,
restless, ravenous they devour the carcass
until only naked bones remain,
the beak pointing to a secret destination,
like some long forgotten signpost
collapsed uselessly upon the ground.

I glance at the humus covered garden floor
where the remnants of what was life
call to the new life that lies beneath,
ready, waiting for its moments in the sun.

Lakeside

Evening descends over the lake
as the last of the sun's rays
ripple across the darkening waters,
the birds are silent in their nests,
and lizards slither under rocks.
I listen to the insistent cicadas
as they sing a song to darkness,
a chill breeze comes to the stillness
while evening leaves rustle
with memories of the day,
and the grass listens silently
to tales of how the men left
as the sun fell noiselessly asleep.
Night-time wraps the place
where glowing animal bones
are monuments to the dead,
in this nocturnal abyss
bats fill the sky, searching for food,
stars are obscured by moonlight
beneath the whispering trees,
creatures of the night are busy.
Then I remember you again,
your memory smells of sweat & salt
from when you fished this lake.
Now by this ancient shore we lie,
separated by time, as memories
sailing towards the distant sea,
slowly peel away the past,
until we, you and me and time,
lost in the night, become as one

Lost

I am of your imagination
I own neither flesh nor form
I'm part of an incomplete puzzle
a creation within your mind
something you cannot turn around
so that I become as real as you
I linger between light and dark
where I imagine you imagine me
there is no escape, no release
from such unending thoughts
so I wander, lost in your mind
just as you wander lost within me
are we dreams or hallucinations
or have we a reality we can't see
that's caught somewhere, waiting
for the end or the beginning
of whatever we might be

Poetry

poetry left me one afternoon
my rhythm and rhyme went away
nothing stirred, not even a leaf
of the notepad I held in my hand
its silence as white as bones
without the flesh of lost words
weighing on it ponderously
my indifference turns pages to dust
dust and shadow—that's all there is
waiting forever to be rearranged
like the words I cannot write

Marking

I mark the passing of the minutes
I mark the passing of the hours
my dark corners grow darker still
as the clouds move with the wind

I mark the passing of the days
I mark the passing of the weeks
the dimness of my nights grows
until even starlight is eclipsed

I mark the passing of the months
I mark the passing of the years
when all the years are ended
I begin again & mark the seconds

Shadow-Cat

shadow-cat prowled the silent streets
where light and darkness fought a war
nothing stirred, but fallen leaves
and the hobo curled up by a door

I watched as darkness shifted slowly
I felt the wind blow cold and raw
along the street her hard eyes flickered
glowing red like hell's own coals

silently the darkness stretched
around, between the moonlit streets
there she stalked the edge of light
the darkest creature of the night

I stood there peering in the stillness
as she stole the pale moonlight
a silent ghost, out seeking prey
a wraith of frost and mist and hate

leaving only her frigid darkness
chilling everything it touched
and her paw-prints faintly glowing
as she walked in winter's frost

Day-Night

Day...
fragments of the sky
came to earth today
reflected the colours
of the world where they fell
sunlight & blue glinted
across the landscape
dreams were caught in trees
lost memories reawakened
my eyes as blue as the sky
mirror my fractured world

Night...
fallen stars are on the ocean
as waves caress my feet
I tread the stardust of dreams
and wonder where daylight is
the moon limns a cloud
casts shadows into the dark
they shift and change
they dance to night's music
becoming shadows of shadows
in darkness where magic dwells

Drought

hot sun pounds on rusting tin roofs
empty street wears an abandoned look
those few still here keep out of the sun
a lunatic wind screams through the town
scorching everything it touches

I feel the tarmac melting under my feet
see sharp-edged shadows all along the street
I glance at the parched world all around
peeling paint and colour faded walls
apart from the wind hardly a sound

this quiet road leads me to another time
when the fields were green and the river ran
children played and laughter echoed
with plenty of food for all to eat—
back before this drought began

now all around is only heat and dust
covering my world with its lifeless pall
the streets, the walls, the shrivelled skin
the memories of bygone years too
when one by one my friends departed

shadows deepen on the scorched walls
I lose myself in their darkness again
I walk along the burning road
I leave this town where I once belonged
and know tonight I'll dream of rain

Moxie

bare trees and evenings
cloudless skies and stars
on the hill a graveyard
forgotten now by history
I follow the lost footprints
that lead to a fallen stone
your memory curls upward
rises as if from a dying fire
a mirage of mist and dew
I move past the stone
past unwanted memories
into the wilderness
of my recollections
mist rises from the ground
from the overgrown grass
like a feeling from yesterday
your memory fades away
echoes from the trees
lead me into the silent night
stars flicker in reassurance
and guide me to where I must be

Museum

you lambent figurine of jade
lying draped in muslin cloth
I admire your silent beauty
as you glow warm and soft
in this museum of dreams
your green colours my skin
as your shadow touches me
I trace your contours
through the muslin shroud
and know we are both refugees
from a distant time and place

your ancient stone glows
merges with my memories
of the city I fled before
I was a ghost in the light
invisible to all but you
the curses we carry
keep us both here
among these dreams
hearing the voices of things
much longer forgotten
even than the years we carry

your veil serves a purpose
and my invisibility too
where light shines through
the darkness remains hidden
and more dreams join us
with each passing night

Nocturne

marvels haunt these woods
among the autumn leaves
bare branches braid the sky
and clutch the clouds
the scent of past seasons
drifts among the trees
as they sing to the dark

a frigid midnight moon
hangs over the dry river
a distant wolf howls
stirring dark fantasies
its call primeval and lost
is answered only by echoes
of its nocturnal loneliness

broken images collide
when white moonlight
fractures the darkness
sand glints and dances
on the dusty riverbed
among those ancient stones
forgotten people left behind

above the jagged tree-line
sketched mountains rise
ethereal like shadows
scratching arcane symbols
among the signalling stars
a dank smell of grief rises
floats like mist in the night

something shifts inside me
my imagination is restless
and as dark shapes move
my eyes open on morning's sky

Reverberations

my silent words
bounce from the walls
and hover in the air
where like dust
they glint in the sun

shifting and dissolving
as memories
settling like snow
drifting to the ground
fragile in their sadness

as they fall they find
new configurations
infinitely complex
that turn my sorrow
into something new

that rises into the air
like a song to new life
an aria born of sorrow
that illuminates the chaos
of my careless life

Farmer

his skin was polished bronze
like a god of the ancient past
sweat glistened on his torso
as he climbed the hillside
in the heat that burdened his day

with a coil of rope on his shoulder
axe in hand father went to work
birds were nervous in the trees
as he paused to catch his breath
then he shrugged and moved on

his shadow danced as he walked
chattering birds rushed into the air
flashed against the cloudless sky
he stopped and swung around
drawn to the sudden raucousness

he dropped the axe near a tree
took the rope from his shoulder
fashioned a loop at one end
tossed it over a thick branch
tied the other end around the trunk

he stood for a few moments
in the dappled shade of the tree
his eyes stared right towards me
but I was invisible amid the trees
where leaves whispered my name

he stared long at the ground
I heard his sobs, his desperation
as his tears fed the ground
then I rushed forward crying too
"no, papa," I shouted, "no, papa"

Leaving

the sun's rays scratch the night-time sky away
a small cloud moves with the blue of morning
the air is filled with the dissonance of birds
as chattering children make their way to school

shadows rise on the white walls of the city
flowers blossom brightly in the vibrant streets
and a cool silence waits inside my room
to catch the sounds of life upon the breeze

I hear words spoken in a language not mine
the mug of coffee grows cold in my hands
its aroma has vanished just as our love did
as the nascent wind took your perfume away

now my bag is packed and ready to go
filled only with sad memories and dust
that will soon be gone as we are done
to never find each other under the sun

I shoulder my backpack as I walk off
and leave no trace that I was ever here
the sun staggers with me along the street
taunting with its warmth the chill I feel

it stretches my shadow until it breaks
while I hear somewhere a raven call
its black black heart on a sunny day
a portent of our dead love foretold

Tree

loneliness is a tree outside my window
its shadow moves like an hour hand
that I want to hold like a thread of hope

I want to untangle what is entwined
in the mass of hanging banyan roots
as they appear to constrict any life

the branches of the tree rise menacingly
a threat perceived but no threat at all
I never close my window on that tree

this tree that shaded me for many summers
the home of my memories and birdsong
that draws all my loneliness into itself

Windows

memories
whisper in the sunlight of morning
a breeze
plays soft music long forgotten
a melody
to accompany insect and birdsong
my windows
I throw open to admit the new day

I embrace
things forgotten in the dark of night
my gaze
wanders to the blue waters of the lake
then moves
to the young lovers sitting idly there
together
they are lost to the world around them

seeing them
they remind me of when I was young
and I wore
your lovers' promise on my finger
together
our life was good from youth to age
until you died
leaving behind my loneliness and loss

and memories
that return with each day's rising sun
to gather
by these windows like house plants

waiting
to be watered by the tears that come
until they bloom
to remind me of the happiness we shared

Soliloquy

tonight the wind sings a requiem
for things that are lost
for those who are gone
the sickle moon hangs in a tree
like a wind-chime making music
the lake is mournful and shadowed
as it waits for morning to come

I walk the shore of pebbles and stones
feeling the pain through my feet
the sky—a black spell of night—watches
as grief unfolds like wings from the land
I feel the lightness of my bones
carrying the heaviness within my heart
night's mist curls up from the world

I think of you across our separation
the bridge from life to death impassable
because life holds me back
I know that night will come again
then I will look for you between the stars
where the emptiness keeps you safe
until we inhabit time and space as one

Streets

the streets are noisy in the light of day
a late autumn mist hangs in the air
and the sharp aromas of cooked food
come from street-stalls and small cafes
I wander these streets—a daily ritual—
seeking answers to puzzles in my life
or sometimes just letting go and shedding
like the fallen leaves all around me
the things I have chosen to leave behind
as I lose myself to find myself
I see young children going off to school
where life's lessons wait to be learned
on the streets I see only strangers—
always strangers hurrying through life—
or lost like me and seeking a way back—
our eyes meet for a fleeting moment
but there is no recognition in their faces
I stop at a tea stall for my morning chai
its jaggery sweetness focuses my mind
and in a revelation as ritual as my walk
I realize that in the century I have known
nothing has changed except the seasons
the songs that echo from radios—
and your heart that once was mine
before my years hung heavy with the
unripe fruit of things that might have been

Dawn

I

night-time has no more songs
the clouds have shed their tears
morning stands at the threshold
waiting for warm sunlight to come
the only sounds are crickets
and the dancing of unseen feet
on the sidewalk of time

II

I watch the morning star in the sky
and wait for long shadows to awaken
and unroll like well-worn prayer mats
pointing to the west where no god is

III

the rhythms of the day tick slowly
amid the songs and the silences of birds
as morning calls upon the world
and children laugh and cry

Unpunctuated

punctuation is like moments in life
when we pause to consider events
scented with our emotions
we sleep as commas or parenthesis
let these small marks echo our lives
I am a hiatus between your thoughts
and you are always a question mark
sometimes we are an endless sentence
with no pause for contemplation
like unending ellipsis for the yet to be
never is there a full stop or a colon
or even a fresh paragraph
waiting to be filled with our words
our lives merge with one another
each day we make choices
whether to continue or pause
whether to break the rules
and surprise ourselves with creativity
wrought in the knowledge
that life is just an exclamation mark
looking for somewhere to rest

Lost Gods

effigies of long forgotten gods
hang on the ancient walls
carved faces blurred by time
their achievements dust

in the sunshine of these ruins
they are nothing but old stone
the world has outgrown them
men, they know, are now gods

their spirits roam these ruins
among the transient tourists
who always fail to understand
that the world was their creation

in each of them something lives—
a heart of stone that still beats
pumping the blood of history
along a line from then to now

only their eyes show they recall
when men worshipped them
and still now, as silence itself
they remember their past

how revered they once were
by those who carved these stones
how the past they brought alive
lives on in the dust of centuries

they stand beneath a desert sky
amid the desolation, they wait
they listen to the ceaseless stars
enduring until their time returns

Vowels

*[A=green, E=blue, I=red, O=black,
U=light & shade]*

A

the fundamental colour of the world—of life
a primal colour—a vowel in cryptic words
a restless chameleon after the rains
semaphores with its many shades
to a fragrant lime tree—laden with fruit
that waits for hands that harvest

E

hands that move through the light of day
collecting the offerings of nature
from the earth and the lime tree
nourished by the natural waters
that flow from the rain-fed rivers
from rain drops to ripe fruit—a full circle

I

the flamboyant sunset that knows
that tomorrow—for a while—it will rule again
absorbing warmth and light until it glows
turning rivers the colour of blood and night
and the limes the colour of verdant soil
filling the air with darkening hues of love

O

the summer sky stretching to the distant sea
darkens as day moves into sombre night
streaks of lightning crackle in the air
compete with the stars to light the world
the heat of day yields to the cooler evening
the lime tree stands limned with silver

U

the cycle of days—of daylight and dark
and the shadows that linger in between
life and love—the finding and the losing
the world's heart—water—limes—the tree
the seasons that give—the seasons that take
all fluctuating between known and unknown

Mud

in the capable hands of the potter
lost memories are worked in clay
and dreams are skilfully shaped
each turn of the wheel, each pot
records a story of love and life
touched, smoothed and formed
until its shape equals its purpose
if form is lost, hands rethrow
the clay and it rises once again
another story, another function
and from mud to near perfection
the ancient clay of the earth
grows into a vessel for living

Reflections

icicles hang from the branches,
gleaming stilettos that melt
in the warmth of the morning sun,
water drops, falling onto the earth,
piercing softly and then are gone,
returned to where they came from—
from the soil to the air to the soil—
unseen after the fall—but never lost,
primordial, eternal, carrying time
and all of life in their fluid wombs,
everything is in each transient drop,
and the illusion of our existence
reflects mirrorlike, but fleetingly

Memories of Snow

it's ages since I saw snow fall
and coat in virgin white
the landscape of solitude
that murmurs with the season

where melancholy trees stand
gaunt like transfixed skeletons
and my dream veils distant hills
in a mist of things remembered

I recall a wood fire burning
with the scent of my homeland
and children who built snowmen—
amorphous figures that changed

like corpses as the snow reddened
from the drops of blood that fell—
then winter was an allegory for loss
of things that can never be again

Night-Watch

the strangeness and mystery of night
its depths of darkness and the light of stars
shadows crouching close to the ground
ominously waiting for fear to hurry by

familiar things take unfamiliar shapes
that are never fixed but always shifting
like candle flames, fireflies come and go
dancing distantly from world-weary eyes

the city stretches up against the sky
gaunt memorial stones to daylight lost
aging walls immovable, transfixed
whose blackness will flee as dawn arrives

mist rises slowly, luminously, over the river
swirls as a winding sheet about the night
birds, captured by the dark, wait patiently
roosting in the places where light never goes

in the deep-shadowed canyons people sleep
their caverns of solitude behind locked doors
around the city, the trees quiver gently
as the autumn leaves sing to the night

under the desolate glow of the moon
that rules the stars, the misty night-time sky
darkness begins to pad its way towards dawn
taking all that is lost into its sombre embrace

The Path

he often spoke of a house in the village,
where happiness played in the silence and light
and birdsong sounded from the great old tree,
its shadow moving to mark passing hours

after school, children lazed by the lily pond,
as vapour trail graffiti traversed the sky,
while he wrote poems in the sprawling shade
and thought about things that had once been

he would close his eyes and breathe deeply,
earth and blossoms now a single aroma
that took him to the house where silence
was as necessary as a summer breeze

sometimes, he could hear the slow tread
of his grandfather's feet as he drew near,
coming to tell familiar tales of other times
on warm afternoons before the winter came

he still carried cold winters in his heart
winters that cooled the warmth of life
until the renewal of springtime arrived
bringing the promise of better days ahead

his mind wandered along a well-worn path
of memories and laughter that led home,
it is a long path but his journey has begun,
and in sunshine or snow the path is clear

Streetlife

on the street with the spice seller's shop
aromas rise like the scent of life itself
as people hurry on private errands

a bangle seller calls out to sell his wares
copper shines in his hands as he promises
god's good fortune to those who buy

men gather at the tea shop drinking chai
nearby a cow sits in the road contemplating
beset by flies it blinks its soulful eyes

women bargain noisily at the grocery shop
for rice and lentils for their hungry families
coins change hands… smiles are like music

pedestrians negotiate the chaos of traffic
that winds through the vibrant town
the market shimmers with festive hues

barefoot children play tag along the street
or run off to fly the plastic kite they bought
they are a whirlwind of non-stop activity

sweating street sellers cook hot food
as delicious odours fill the coming night
strings of lights begin to twinkle like fireflies

laughter and singing are heard everywhere
as the ghost of happiness comes to play
and will stay like a dream until the sun rises

Night Ballad

have you watched the night sky
have you seen the stars move
did you hear the night train whistle
is cold coffee on the stove

will your turntable play
your favourite melody
will the music that you hear
make you think of me

as the moon lights the contours
of your recumbent form
as the night jasmine fills
the night with its perfume

open wide your window
to admit the jasmine air
to let the fragrance mingle
with the fragrance of your hair

sing a line from a song
that awakens memories
that travel through the night
to the ebony painted trees

through the parted curtains
through which the night can hear
the music of your love
so very loud and clear

then hurry to meet me
in your sleep or wide awake
where we'll wander, lose our way
wherever we may be

or ride the whistling train
into the plangent night
into magic and stardust
that takes us to our dreams

Morning

sunshine calms the stormy sky
as a bird comes to my window
and taps its code against the glass
to remind me of the forgotten
and of the half remembered—
things lost in the light of day

I sit there gazing upon the world
through eyes that seek yesterday
while the breeze duets with time
and children chant old rhymes
I whistle a tune from my childhood
as the bird blinks and flies away

opening the doors to the quiet light
I smell the sunshine and the air
my arms embrace our shared sky
unspoken words flood into me—
the story of the hours to come—
and finally I remember

Seasons (1)

winter's wind blows long and hard
the cold curling shadows dark
the mist drapes the bare trees
as snow swirls in the backyard

footsteps move soundlessly
grey skies light the woodland path
and yet the winter roses bloom
dispelling the pall of gloom

underneath the snowy bed
nature sleeps, not yet dead
spring shall again the beauty bring
as new leaves will see the red

the mist and gloom will fade away
birdsongs then will fill the day
snow and shadows will reveal
all that the winter had concealed

During the writing of these collaborations we both produced a version of what we thought the finished poem should be and then selected the one we both preferred. Occasionally we coudn't agree; in those few cases we give both versions here.

Seasons (2)

winter's wind blows long and hard
cold curling in dark shadows
snowflakes swirl in our backyard

freezing mist enfolds bare trees
twists among the mouldering leaves
footsteps moving soundlessly

dull skies lighting woodland paths
but yet the winter roses bloom
and cast their colour in the gloom

now flushed with roseate hues
that show that nature is not dead
as new leaves soon will see red

mist and gloom will pass away
snow and shadows will reveal
ending then our wintry days

During the writing of these collaborations we both produced a version of what we thought the finished poem should be and then selected the one we both preferred. Occasionally we coudn't agree; in those few cases we give both versions here.

Monochrome (1)

last night I saw a black and white movie
lives caught between shadow and light
in a past that vanished before I existed
a familiar world—and yet so strange

I imagined my father's face in a crowd
(but then everyone looked so much alike
with their trilby hats and collars turned)
for just a moment he was alive again

then he was gone—a vanished illusion
a play of light in the moving shadows
that exist between white and black
where celluloid ghosts are immortal

scenes flashed and flickered before me
with their precisely sculpted dialogue
sounding flat and one dimensional
in the monochrome of my night

through eighty minutes I watched
hoping my father would walk again
on the colourless streets of the past
where the credits must finally roll

During the writing of these collaborations we both produced a version of what we thought the finished poem should be and then selected the one we both preferred. Occasionally we coudn't agree; in those few cases we give both versions here.

Monochrome (2)

in a black & white movie last night
lives were caught in forgotten time
a past as shadowy as my childhood
now inaccessible, illusory & distant

I saw my father's face in a crowd
a memory given fleeting life
he was a phantom of light & dark
there for a moment & then gone

grainy scenes flickered & flashed
twenty-four frames in a second
I wanted to rewind & see again
that face I had almost forgotten

sounds & sights now faded & gone
my father's voice calling me home
but all I found was a lingering fog
in which both time & I were lost

During the writing of these collaborations we both produced a version of what we thought the finished poem should be and then selected the one we both preferred. Occasionally we couldn't agree; in those few cases we give both versions here.

Stories

tales we tell no one
that are ours to keep
phantasms of words
**haunting our thoughts
starting, ending
going somewhere else**

larger than life
larger than we imagine
there is no escape
as they define our lives
our labyrinth of woes
our mountains of hope

every day they are new
they are our homes
and the roads we walk
they reflect our fears
they reflect our joys
they fill lonely days

they come to know us
as we discover them
together we cry, we laugh
we invent and reinvent
new secret stories
ours to keep, to tell no one

Still Life (1)

a summer afternoon
a still life painting
a vase of flowers
casts a deep shadow
not a speck of breeze
disturbs the scene
memory glints like dust
in lattices of light
gilding the edges
of lilacs & roses
I hold their fragrance
the aroma of oils & inks
the whiff of your smoke
the rain soaked silence
outside my dusty window
emptiness is in my palm
but beauty is in my heart
I nudge open my window
& watch the clouds dispel

During the writing of these collaborations we both produced a version of what we thought the finished poem should be and then selected the one we both preferred. Occasionally we couldn't agree; in those few cases we give both versions here.

Still Life (2)

a quiet afternoon
a still life painting
a vase of flowers
a deep shadow
not a hint of breeze
disturbs the scene
as dusty memories
glint in the light
of my imagination
gilding the edges
of lilies and roses

my reverie deep
I dream eyes open
I grasp intangibles
holding the aroma
of oils and inks
rain soaked silences
the beauty inside me
forever kept safe
I open my windows
and hear soft laughter
as the clouds dispel

During the writing of these collaborations we both produced a version of what we thought the finished poem should be and then selected the one we both preferred. Occasionally we coudn't agree; in those few cases we give both versions here.

Coadunation

her dark skin glistening with sweat
she stood like an alabaster statue
in the shadows of the deserted temple
tresses flowing over her breasts
a string of skulls around her neck
her eyes like dying embers of fire
her forehead painted crimson
she looked striking in red and black
those eternal hues of sin and lust

from a corner of that quiet place
I watched her morning rituals begin
her strong form moving gracefully
as her goddess waited behind her
smeared with symbolic vermilion
until the homage of flesh to stone
and the dark and ancient ritual
signifying birth, love and death
brought the merging of their blood

Stone Ghosts

I reach out and touch the walls,
feel marks on crumbling stones,
wonder where the people went
who once made this their home

while these ruins whisper tales
of life and loss in ancient times,
deep sorrow clings to them
like vines eclipsing history

they drink the echoes of the past,
in torpid, hot afternoon sun
that I feel burn upon my back,
as this place weeps its loneliness

I heard the murmur of my heart
when I came to this desert ruin,
long-dead voices called to me
from unremembered walls

now I watch the orphaned stones,
as like sentinels they sit,
in silence undead dreams still linger,
but find no resolution now

pale ghosts emerge between the walls,
then disappear into my thoughts,
as fine dust settles in the stony cracks,
and night-time drags me slowly home

Wondering

I sit on the bridge and wonder
about things I don't understand
until I realise that understanding
is not needed, wondering is enough
then I wonder about wondering
so my thoughts move in circles
I feel there is a universe within me
so large it has nowhere to go
it is filled with all things
everything that ever was or will be
my thoughts find another reality
that is so familiar, and yet so strange
the line between the two
is whisper thin and endlessly wide
here roads become rivers
and clouds become flowers
mountains turn to sand dunes
fish fly above the earth
stars hang suspended from trees
only one thing remains unchanged
the bridge where I sit and wonder
although I don't believe in god
I think that maybe I am god
if that's so I must believe in myself
so now I must prove that I exist
as the world changes around me
I feel my presence, I know I exist—
now I must wonder about that

Chiaroscuro

the penumbra of my shadow fades to light,
in the quiet of autumn the river awakes,
the sky's night-time tears lie in puddles,

distant mountains rise—ethereal visions
creating a union between heaven and Earth,
beyond them, the blood-like sun tints the sky

as it claws its gradual way towards morning,
I stand here, collecting early fragrances
from wild flowers that open with the dawn,

I gather too, the leaves of past autumns,
those fragile and distant memories,
whose echoes I hear sighing in the breeze

dancing with dust along the village street,
I find my voice in the shadows of sunrise
and bid good morning to a new-born day.

Pavane

midnight lingers in a city without sleep,
bats dance with stars in the moonlit air,
I watch shadows curl beneath streetlights
and listen to the songs of deepest night;
in lonely lanes night creatures prowl,
their furtiveness a soundless requiem

a silhouette appears along the street,
a dark shape grows out of the night,
more shapes are born and then a voice,
a siren call enticing from the void;
I keep silent as I watch, not to intrude
on this covert pageant of dark and light

they pass, an endless blur of blackest black,
that dances a pavane with time itself,
I whistle a refrain, now half forgotten,
an aria that makes merry with the gloom,
my memories fall like dead autumn leaves,
scatter silently in the midnight breeze

the moon shines cold and unconcerned,
cats call from their dark alleyways;
shrinking from the throng of spectres,
alone, surrounded by the night,
midnight it seems for me may never pass,
but somewhere I can imagine day

Alphabet Soup

I have this pile of unused words
I thought I'd turn them into a story
string them together somehow
but I'm lacking all punctuation
without commas & periods
my words look forlorn & naked

so I sort them by meaning
into smaller piles of words
none of which are sentences
yet they're so profound, complete
that I give them away like blessings
less meaningful words remain

the space left reinvents itself
waits for more words to arrive
simple words keep their distance
from more complex words
the simple words are like slaves
there is no amity between the two

the meaningful words are used first
simple words are again unused
I try joining them together
but they just don't make sense
they're good only for alphabet soup
it's the 'special' on the menu today

Seascape

the tears that I left
in the sand by the sea
have turned to salty brine
part of the ocean, part of me
the tears of the earth
that must forever be

the sea that took you away
I watched with dead eyes
you went with the waves
you went with the weed
I never said goodbye
so I stood here and cried

Desolation

the city's trees are dying
the streets are canyon hot
a stink of summer fills the air
carnage… flies and rot
the sky is ashen grey
as thin as old men's hair
I've watched this city moult
until it's deathly bare
the river has grown old
it's turned as thick as mud
what lies beneath is dead
no heart to pump the blood
what lies above stagnates
and withers in the sun
now they're cutting trees
the slaughter has begun
the chainsaw's noisy whine
drowns out the cries of trees
when they are all cut down
there'll be no more of these
soon the city will be naked
but for concrete… brick & stone
dehumanised… unliveable
where then will be our homes

Stardust

when gilded lilies sleep at night
she tiptoes in the quiet garden
her hair—a moonlit comet tail
her scent—of bygone things
she looks up to the evening stars
forget-me-nots she calls them
for each one is a memory

a shooting star lights the sky
then extinguishes like yesterday
stretching open her small hands
smiling at the stardust she carries—
it glistens brightly—her feet
carry her swiftly, noiselessly
as she vanishes among the trees

Daybreak

in the half light of dawn
as the day comes gradually alive
she winds her hair into a bun
secures it with a wooden pin
tiptoes onto the shaded veranda
and smiles at the morning sky

beside the well, water jugs wait
to be filled and carried home
she sweeps fallen leaves into a heap—
litter from the night-time wind—
then hums quietly to herself
as she lights the mud-walled stove

inside she hears a charpoy creak
soon her home will fill with sounds
as her children come awake
like a ghost she scurries around
doing things that must be done
her duties heavy on her mind

as her day is given to others
a breeze stirs the champa tree
scented flowers twist to the ground
grass and leaves whisper to her
calling her thoughts to the river
where water flows forever free

www.ingramcontent.com/pod-product-compliance
Lightning Source LLC
LaVergne TN
LVHW041549070426
835507LV00011B/1003